Rio Vista
Through Time

PHILIP PEZZAGLIA

America Through Time®
ADDING COLOR TO AMERICAN HISTORY

This book is dedicated to my wife and children, for being so very patient and supportive while I poured over boxes of photographs researching and compiling information for this project.

America Through Time is an imprint of Fonthill Media LLC
www.through-time.com
office@through-time.com

Published by Arcadia Publishing by arrangement with Fonthill Media LLC
For all general information, please contact Arcadia Publishing:
Telephone: 843-853-2070
Fax: 843-853-0044
E-mail: sales@arcadiapublishing.com
For customer service and orders:
Toll-Free 1-888-313-2665

www.arcadiapublishing.com

First published 2019

ISBN 978-1-63500-096-2

Typeset in Mrs Eaves XL Serif Narrow
Printed and bound in England

INTRODUCTION

Since the community of Rio Vista was settled in 1858, it has suffered devastation from both flood waters and fire. Due to floodwaters, the town was forced to relocate when just four years old. When Rio Vista was just thirty years old, at its present location, a devastating fire wiped out much of the downtown. Each time the community banded together, rebuilt, and moved forward, chalking the events up to experience.

As Rio Vista grew from a small community that's primary industry was fishing into a more agricultural-oriented community, its growth and goings-on often made the community newsworthy and the center of attention.

Whether it was the explosion of the steamship *Yosemite*, the establishment of two prestigious academies, a nationally-known asparagus cannery, the filming of silent movies, the discovery of natural gas, the invention of the sugar beet harvester, the construction of a bridge awarded the "American Institute of Steel Construction's Annual Award of Merit for the Most Beautiful Steel Bridge Class IV," or the misdirected whales—Humphrey, Delta, and Dawn—one thing is for sure, Rio Vista is a unique town with a fascinating past.

Located at the tip of Solano County, the community of Rio Vista is one of the oldest in the county. Its position on the Sacramento River approximately at the halfway point between San Francisco and Sacramento made it a historically significant point during the early days of steamship travel and the establishment of the communities of the Delta.

The initial establishment of Rio Vista began when John Bidwell's 17,752-acre land grant known as Rancho Los Ulpinos was sold off on December 3, 1855. Colonel Nathan H. Davis purchased six of the twenty tracts that day, which fronted the Sacramento River, for a total of $440.

Colonel Davis purchased the acreage with the intent to subdivide part of the land into a town, and in the fall of 1857, he surveyed a plat, on lot no. 3, for a town. The site that he chose for the settlement was approximately one mile below the mouth of Cache Slough and he named it "Los Brazos del Rio" (Arms of the River) because it was situated so near the three branches of the Sacramento River.

Once the surveying was done, he set off to persuade pioneers to settle in his new town. It may have begun slowly but once the word was out, the settlement grew rapidly, and fishing became the prime industry. Robert C. Carter and his son established a salmon cannery, which would ship salmon daily to San Francisco and from that point internationally. Before long the community boasted two general stores, a butcher shop, two hotels, a blacksmith shop, drug store, livery stable, and tin shop as well as a handful of private residences owned a by pioneers with the names of Davis, Sidwell, Squires, Bryant, Perry, Westgate, Fallman, Freeman, Carter, Dunham, and Hammel.

In the spring of 1858, Col. Davis hired John Sidwell to construct a wharf 75 feet long and 24 feet wide. Following its construction, Col. Davis petitioned for a post office, which would force the steamer *New World*, which carried mail, to make daily stops; however, when petitioning for a post office, it was approved with the provision that the name of the settlement be changed to a less Spanish sounding name. Mrs. Mary Kirkpatrick, wife of Charles, who would become the postmaster, chose the name "Rio Vista" (*La Vista del Rio*, in correct Spanish), which means "River View," and it was quickly adopted.

In 1859, the California Transportation Company leased the wharf and doubled its size, thus making it possible for additional steamers, such as the *Senator*, *Antelope*, and *Eclipse* to make daily stops, just as the *New World* was already doing.

For the next couple of years, Rio Vista was a thriving village with Salmon fishing, a paying industry, engaging numerous men, and becoming the settlements leading industry.

During the final days of December 1861, Rio Vista experienced high winds and heavy rains, during which the waters of the mighty Sacramento River swelled and overflowed, onto the lowlands, with the waters rising high enough that it washed away many of the smaller buildings in the settlement. But these villagers were a seasoned close-knit group who had helped one another through the hardships, which they had endured during the previous winters. Those with lost property were quickly brought into the homes of the more fortunate. As the townspeople watched nature take its course, they realized that there was little or nothing that they could do to prevent the impending storms.

The height of these storms arrived on January 9, 1862. It was on this day that a great storm hit the delta town, bringing with it a fierce wind from the southeast and a heavy surplus of rain. This lethal combination of the wind and the rain caused the river to rise over the banks and into the town. The floodwaters were as high as twelve feet at the foot of Main Street, and before long, the entire town was under water. Those who lived through the flood remarked that for as many miles as the eye could see, the lands were covered with water.

Two months later, in March of 1862, Samuel R. Perry, John M. Sidwell, William K. Squires, and Issac Dunham, from the former Rio Vista settlement, went to see Mr. Joseph Bruning, a wealthy rancher, who lived a league down river from the Rio Vista settlement, on a higher plat of the land grant, located on an upper edge of the Montezuma Hills. Bruning had previously been in the hotel business in San Francisco, when due to ill

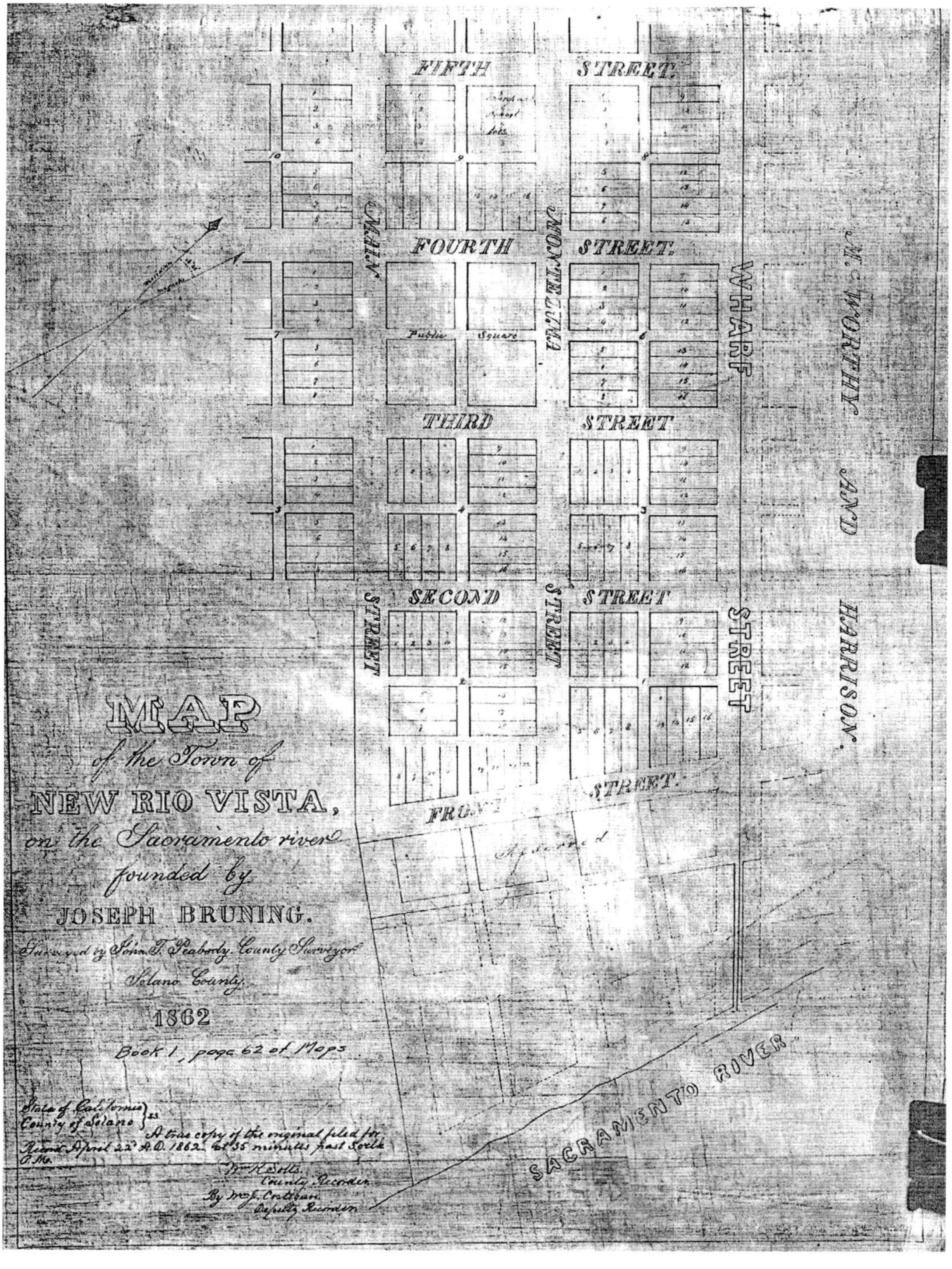

FIFTH STREET
FOURTH STREET
THIRD STREET
SECOND STREET
FRONT STREET
MAIN STREET
MONTEZUMA STREET
WHARF STREET
Mc WORTHY AND HARRISON.
Public Square
SACRAMENTO RIVER
MAP
of the Town of
NEW RIO VISTA,
on the Sacramento river
founded by
JOSEPH BRUNING.
Surveyed by John T. Peabody County Surveyor
Solano County.
1862
Book 1, page 62 of Maps

health he purchased land in the Los Ulpinos grant, around 1858. The four former Rio Vista residents asked Joseph Bruning if he would be willing to sell them a plot of land on which to rebuild the Rio Vista settlement. Mr. Bruning granted their request, but refused payment; instead, he gave them gave them the land on the northeastern part of his property. Accordingly, Bruning surveyed and recorded the town plat of "New Rio Vista" in March 1862. T. J. McWorthy, who owned the property, adjacent to the northern edge of Bruning's, also surveyed and recorded an addition to the town.

This "new" Rio Vista grew quite rapidly and a handful of the people from the old settlement relocated to start again. Hotels and stores were established. S. R. Perry erected the first store. J. M. Sidwell put up a hotel, on Second Street, as did Wm. K. Squires on South Front Street. The post office was established at Samuel R. Perry's store, located on the southwest corner of Main and Front Streets with Mr. Perry assuming the position of postmaster, a position that he had held in the old settlement. Robert Carter & son built another small salmon cannery, which they operated, on north Front Street, until 1865, when Robert Jr. opened a tin store.

Just as had been done in "old" Rio Vista, one of the first orders of business for the new town was to construct a wharf, which Joseph Bruning built in the spring of 1862. Bruning sold the wharf to the Steam Navigation Co. and eventually, California Pacific R. R. Co. owned it.

As more individuals settled in Rio Vista, many of which were immigrants, farming became the way of life rather than fishing. Immigrants from Germany, Portugal, England, Sweden, Scotland, and Canada, to name but a few, each educated in their native lands, brought to the community new ideas, which were combined to create fertile crops and a diverse community.

Following the establishment of Rio Vista, at its current location, the remaining four decades of the nineteenth century saw the community experiencing many events which shaped the town. Most notable was the opening of the first public school, in 1862; the explosion of the steamship *Yosemite*, in 1865; the establishment of St. Joseph's Catholic Parish, the First Congregational Church of Rio Vista and the Methodist Church; the establishment of St. Gertrude's Academy for Girls, in 1876; the establishment of local newspapers; the *Weekly Gleaner*, *Rio Vista Enterprise*, and *Sacramento River News* (later renamed the *River News*), in 1890; the downtown fire of 1892; and the incorporation of Rio Vista, in 1893.

Both the *Yosemite* disaster and the opening of St. Gertrude's Academy for Girls brought attention to the fledging community of Rio Vista. The *Yosemite* became front page news on *Harper's Weekly* and was reported in most of the Northern California newspapers as one of the worst steamship disasters of the era.

Thirty years after the devastating flood of 1862, Rio Vista was once again stricken with disaster. On the morning of July 20, 1892, Miss Emily Dobbins discovered flames in the rear of the second floor of the River View Hotel. The hotel stood on the corner of Main and Second Streets, where the present Rio Vista Hotel stands. Miss Dobbins ran screaming down the hotel stairs and out into the street, gaining the attention of several men who ran into the building and turned on the hotel fire hose; unfortunately, the hose was dry.

With a north wind and the fact that most of the building's downtown were wooden buildings, within minutes the flames spread, eventually destroying practically every business from Front Street up to Third Street, and from Montezuma Street to Sacramento Street.

In just three hours, some seventy-five residences, sheds, and business buildings were destroyed, eighteen families were rendered homeless, and 200,000 dollars' worth of damages went up in flames.

The merchants of town announced their plans of rebuilding the downtown almost immediately after the fire. The community was strong and willing to work hard, showing the same determination that many of the pioneers showed after the flood of 1862. Of course, this time around, having seen the damage fire had on wooden buildings, many of the new buildings were constructed out of brick.

This was truly one of the saddest days in Rio Vista's history, but if there had been any lesson learned, it was that the city needed a better water works system and firefighting equipment. The only foreseeable way that this was to happen was the incorporation of Rio Vista.

After two decades of local debate, it was finally decided that it was in the best interest of the community to incorporate. Thus, the town of Rio Vista held its first election, and the community became officially incorporated on December 30, 1893.

Of the Rio Vista population of approximately 650, only 129 were eligible voters, and of the 129 eligible voters, only 119 turned out. The results of the election votes were fifty-nine for incorporation and forty-six against.

In 1903, St. Joseph's Academy for Boys established as a companion to the already twenty-five-year-old St. Gertrude's Academy for Girls. Once again, Rio Vista was the talk of the Bay Area, as word spread quickly of a fine residence school for boys that was too be run in conjunction with St. Gertrude's Academy. St. Gertrude's, which had been decreasing in enrollment, was closed in 1930, followed by the closure of St. Joseph's in 1932.

The first discussions of a bridge being built across the Sacramento River at Rio Vista, joining the mainland with the fertile islands to the east as well as connecting Solano County with Sacramento County, occurred in 1914. Four years later, construction began on the original bascule bridge, and was completed in January of 1919, with Solano and Sacramento Counties sharing the $260,000 cost. The new bridge linked the town of Rio Vista with the "newly" constructed River Road, on the eastern shore. At this point in time, plans were being made for a future highway heading to Sacramento, following the river, while plans were also being made to better the road between Rio Vista and Suisun also.

In 1933, the idea for a fishing "derby" was originated by two newspapermen, Phil Rose of Redwood City and Harry Proctor of Oakland. The men had the idea of holding a "bass fishing derby" at Rio Vista, to try and increase interest in the sport of fishing. The first annual Striped Bass Derby was held for two consecutive Sundays in the middle of

December 1933. The event was deemed a success and within a short time the chamber was making plans for the second one.

The Derby was held until 1938, when it went on hiatus for a decade, and was resurrected in 1949, by local merchant Romildo "Braid" Pezzaglia, for what many people consider to be the first "official" Rio Vista Bass Derby of the modern era.

Probably the most notable event of the twentieth century, which had a significant impact in all avenues of Rio Vista life, was the discovery of natural gas in 1936. It had been speculated for several years that there might be the presence of oil in the Rio Vista-Montezuma Hills area. During the 1920s, several teams of geologists inspected the area and exploratory wells were drilled in 1921 and 1928. Unfortunately, the wells met with negative results. However, on June 18, 1936, just two miles west of town, the Amerada Petroleum Corporation brought in the first producing well. When the wildcat initially went up, Amerada was drilling for oil, when instead they discovered natural gas. The history making well would be christened "Emigh No. 1."

The gas industry created an unexpected employment and a housing boom in Rio Vista. Besides drilling companies, the need for more trucking firms, welders, tool companies, fabricators, hotels, etc. increased. As more wells were drilled, more employment was created, money made, and Rio Vista began to reap the benefits.

Over the course of 160 years, Rio Vista has been recognized as a small town with a very rich history, unique in so many ways that it is hard to fully summarize in a handful of photographs and accompanying words; nonetheless, I will try. As the town embraces the twenty-first century and continues to grow, its humble beginnings must not be forgotten. The intention of this book is to give the reader an idea of how Rio Vista once looked. Some photographs will show many changes, while others will depict how things have remained the same.

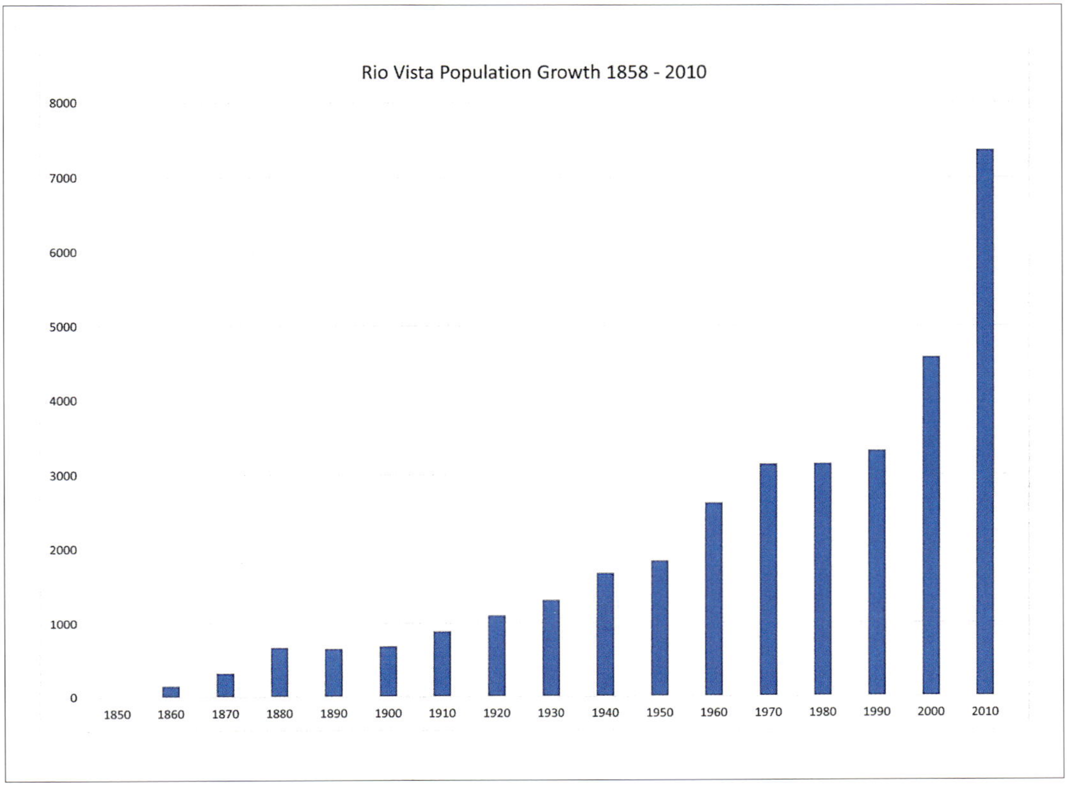

CENSUS CHART AND DATA 1858-2010: The population/census graphs, compiled by the author, show the growth of Rio Vista and Solano County, from 1860 to the present. At the time of the flood of 1862, the original settlement of Rio Vista, founded four years earlier by N. H. Davis, had a population of approximately 150. The increased growth after 2000 can be contributed to the building of the Homecoming, Vineyard Bluffs, and Summerset (later renamed Trilogy) housing subdivisions.

Population / Census
Comparison Chart 1850 - 2010

	1850	**1860**	**1870**	**1880**	**1890**	**1900**	**1910**	**1920**	**1930**
Rio Vista		150	319	666	648	682	884	1104	1309
Solano County	580	7160	16871	18475	20946	24143	27559	40602	40834
California	92597	379994	560247	864694	1213398	1485053	2377549	3426861	5677251
United States	23191876	31443321	39818449	50189209	62947714	76212168	92228496	106021537	122775046

	1940	**1950**	**1960**	**1970**	**1980**	**1990**	**2000**	**2010**	**2020**
Rio Vista	1666	1831	2616	3135	3142	3316	4571	7360	
Solano County	49118	104843	134579	171909	235203	340421	394542	413344	
California	6907387	10586223	15717204	19953134	23667902	29760021	33871648	37253956	
United States	132164569	151325798	179323175	203302031	226545805	248709873	281421906	308700000	

MAIN STREET 1874/2018: The earliest photograph of Main Street Rio Vista, taken around 1874, possibly as early as 1869, and looking towards the Sacramento River, shows the township to be made up of a handful of buildings and a dirt road leading to a wharf at the foot of the street, where a steamship is docked. Pictured on the right, of the photograph, stands the prominent two-story brick building erected on the southwest corner of Main and Second Streets, by Joseph Bruning.

SQUIRES HOTEL 1869 & 1878 ADVERTISEMENT: The top photograph, taken in 1869, shows the Squires Hotel, established by William Squires, in 1862. The hotel, located on Front Street, one block off Main Street, was the second hotel built in "new" Rio Vista. Squires had preciously erected a hotel in "old" Rio Vista in 1859, operating it until it was destroyed during the devastating downtown fire of 1862. During its latter years, the hotel was known as the "Russ House."

SQUIRE'S HOTEL,

Front street, Between Main and Montezuma,

RIO VISTA.

WM. K. SQUIRES, - - - - Proprietor.

This House is FIRST-CLASS in every respect, and every attention paid to the comfort of the guests. Hunting parties will find this just the House for them, as the Proprietor is an old hunter and familiar with all the Hunting Grounds in this section.

There is a Bar and Billlard Table in connection with the House.

BOARD BY THE WEEK AT REASONABLE RATES.

WM. K. SQUIRES.

HOTEL RIVERVIEW 1907 AND F & M BANK 2018: The Squires Hotel was torn down and the Hotel Riverview was erected in its place during the 1890s. Peter Heringer was the proprietor of the hotel when this photo was taken. Citizens Utilities purchased the property and replaced the old hotel with their office building. When the utility company closed their customer service office, the building remained vacant, until the Bank of Rio Vista moved its bookkeeping department into it, eventually adding a second floor.

FRANK BACHASSON AND COMPANY/RIO VISTA SANITATION 2019: The Barberi Brothers operated one of the most popular saloons in Rio Vista during the late 1800s. When the brothers tired of the business, they sold their building, in May 1891, to Frank Bachasson and his nephew, Peter Cattey, who continued the business under the name Frank Baschasson and Company. Later, the building was sold to Joseph and Serpa, who conducted the same type of business.

CHASE'S GENERAL MERCHANDISE STORE 1907 FLOOD / LUCY'S CAFÉ 2019: James Chase initially opened his general merchandise store, on the corner of Main and Front Streets, during the early 1860s. That building was destroyed during the fire of 1892, and he commissioned a new structure to be built, for the same purpose, on the same site. That second structure was torn down during the early 1930s. This image, taken in 1907, depicts the high flood waters which caused havoc on many of the early merchants of Rio Vista.

MAIN STREET CIRCA 1910 AND 1926: Looking west, up Main Street, this *circa* 1910 photograph reveals, at left (south), the Cobweb Saloon, J. T. Brown, unknown, Allendar Building, McGraugh Building, and on the corner of Main and Second Streets, J. Stern & Co. On the north side, the businesses of Joseph & Serpa Dealers in Wines & Liquors, on the corner of Front and Main Streets; the offices of the *River News* and the two-story Union Hall, are visible.

MAIN STREET 1939 AND 2018: In 1939, the first two blocks of Main Street contained many businesses, including Mendes Place, the *River News*, Jess's Café, Bank of Rio Vista, Gordon-Hansen Company, and Fosters. By the end of 2018, only Fosters and the *River News* were still in business, Fosters in the same location and the *River News* having been relocated to South Front Street, in the 1960s. Front Street businesses visible are Ben F. Willis's Super Service Station, Pereira's Groceries, and A. R. Cavagnaro's Blacksmith Shop.

INTERSECTION OF MAIN AND FRONT STREETS 1899 & BANK OF RIO VISTA 1929: The First National Bank of Rio Vista opened on November 1, 1915. The $20,000 two-story reinforced concrete structure featured an exterior of pressed brick with columns and ornamentations of terra cotta. The upper floor featured two office rooms and two apartments, while the lower floor housed the bank. After the Bank of Rio Vista purchased controlling shares of stock of their competitor in 1921, they merged the two banks, and moved into the First National's building.

Bank of Rio Vista 1950s/F & M Bank 2018: Originally the banks rooms on the first floor were finished in mahogany with lobby floors and wainscot finished in Italian marble. During the mid-1950s, the Bank of Rio Vista purchased the adjacent Gordon-Hansen building and enlarged the bank, doubling its size. The remodel included the modernization of the exterior façade of both buildings to make it look as one, as well as the removal of the rear section to create a parking lot.

Red and White Store 1940s/Pets 4 All 2018: The Red and White Store, located in the western most storefront of the Allender building in the 100 block of Main Street, was originally opened by Edward F. Brazil in the 1930s. Around 1940, Norris Ralph Pezzaglia purchased the business and continued its operation until 1948. A portion of Allenders Ice Cream Parlor, which was also the local bus stop, can be seen to the left.

ALLENDER BUILDING 1968 & 2018: The Allender building is the second oldest building on Main Street and was erected immediately following the downtown fire of 1892. Originally, the building consisted of three separate store fronts, each measuring 20' x 50'. The front section of the eastern most storefront was destroyed by fire during the late 1960s while it was being occupied by the Rio Vista Bakery, owned and operated by the Yorg Brothers. Presently, the building houses a barber shop, restaurant, and pet store.

MAIN STREET 1929/1976: Looking down Main Street in 1929, the south side of the 100 block was occupied by (left to right) Bank of Rio Vista, Brown & Gordon Co., the *Rio Vista Banner* (newspaper), E. O. Miller's Jewelry Store, Foster's Club, Unknown, and Yorg Bros. Home Town Bakery (McGraugh-Allender Building). The bottom image was taken in 1976, during one of the few snow storms in local history. The Bank of Rio Vista and Fosters were the only businesses operating in both years.

DOWNTOWN LIGHTING 1962/DOWNTOWN 2018: The top photograph was taken during an evening in June 1962, primarily to showcases the new downtown street lights; however, the image also captures the local businesses of the day: Hap's Bait and Tackle, the Hansen Building (containing automotive and laundry businesses) on the north side, while the south side of the street included: Jessen's Café, warehouse (formerly P. G. & E.), and city hall. The Jessen's building was constructed in 1927, replacing the old Chase building.

McGraugh Building: Located on the corner of Main and Second Streets is the McGraugh Building, sometimes referred to historically as the Simpson-McGraugh Building. The building has housed numerous businesses, including several barbershops (operated by Lamb, Hudson and Foord); saloons and bars, a casino, jeweler, insurance and real estate offices, and currently, a book store. Several scenes for the 1974 film *The McCullochs* were filmed in the building, when it was the "Wagon Wheel."

RIO VISTA HORSE SHOW PARADE & FEBRUARY 2019: The backdrop of this parade scene, from 1915 or '16, is Union Hall (a.k.a. the Gibson Building), located on the northeast corner of Main and Front Streets. For many years, the bottom portion of the building was occupied by Claude Kagee's Billiard and Pool Hall-Soft Drink Emporium, a very popular and frequented local establishment. In February 1905, celebrated author Jack London presented a lecture on socialism to a less-than-enthusiastic crowd. The building was destroyed by fire in 1927.

HOTEL RIO VISTA 1940S & TODAY: During the 1940s, the ground floor of the Hotel Rio Vista included several businesses: The Creamery, Rio Vista Tavern, Pezzaglia's Toggery, and Barry Pharmacy. Several years after the Gibson Building was destroyed, a new building was constructed in its place, occupied by Western Auto Supply Company in the largest store front, with a clothing store, beauty parlor, and barber on the South Second Street side, and Schafer's Ben Franklin Store in the adjacent Main Street storefront.

MAIN AND SECOND STREETS PRE-1926 & 2018: Since the time that the top photograph was taken, between 1919-1926, Rio Vista's Main Street has changed little other than the businesses that occupy the buildings. The earlier image captures a normal day in the life of Rio Vista, highlighting J. Stern & Co., Isham, Vista Theater, Cardoza Building, Hotel Rio Vista (Hite Pharmacy), and Union Baptist Church. The only building missing in the current image is the two-story automotive building, which was torn down in the mid-1960s.

WEBER'S FEDERATED STORE 1940S & PIZZA FACTORY 2018: Since 1892, the following businesses have operated out of the building on the southwest corner of Main and Second streets: J. Stern & Co. 1892-1942; Weber's Federated Store 1942-1988; The Pizza Factory 1988-current. LeRoy Weber Sr. and his son opened Weber's Federated Store in 1942 and continued to operate out of this storefront until 1988, when they relocated to 150 Main Street. The building is considered the oldest on Main Street.

4TH OF JULY PARADE AND MAIN STREET 2019: The former brick Bank of Rio Vista building is the only building featured in both photographs. When the bank relocated in 1921, Murray Isham's Rio Vista Transit Co. moved into their former building. The livery stable was replaced with the Vista Theater in 1925, and on the vacant lot, which was once the site of a blacksmith shop, the Cardoza Building was constructed in 1927. The theater continued to operate, under several proprietorships, until it closed its doors in 1974.

200 BLOCK OF MAIN STREET 1930s & 2009: This 1930s view of Main Street, looking east, shows the 200 blocks businesses of Sol Mogel's drug store (Cardoza Building), Vista Theatre and J. Stern and Company. Farther down, in the next block, Foord's Casino; the Bank of America; and, at the end of the block, the Bank of Rio Vista, are visible. By 2009, when the lower image was taken, the businesses had changed; nonetheless, all the buildings remain.

WEEKLY RIO VISTA GLEANER.

VOL. III. RIO VISTA, SOLANO CO., SATURDAY, SEPTEMBER 7, 1878. No. 1

RIO VISTA ENTERPRISE.

VOLUME I. RIO VISTA, SOLANO COUNTY, CAL., SATURDAY, SEPTEMBER 29, 1877. NUMBER 2.

WEEKLY RIO VISTA GLEANER 1878/*RIO VISTA ENTERPRISE* 1877: The first local newspaper in Rio Vista was *Rio Vista Weekly Gleaner*, owned and operated by Lyman Luther Palmer from September 1877 through February 1879. From April 1878, until its closing, its offices were in Dan McGraugh's Saloon, on the Southeast corner of Main and Second Streets. The *Rio Vista Enterprise* was printed under the direction of proprietors-publishers, John Whitman and W. A. Bushnell, from their offices at the corner of Main and Third Streets, from September 1877 through May 1879.

SHELL SERVICE STATION & CURRENT PARKING LOT: The Shell Service station was constructed on the northeast corner of Main and Third Streets, during the 1930s, by Mr. McKinnon. The station, along with the two-story Abel Chevrolet building, was torn down in 1966 to make way for the new Bank of America building and parking lot. The bank relocated from 138 Main Street, and remained in the new building until it closed, and the Bank of Stockton moved in.

MASONIC HALL 1880S/HOTEL FIRE 1917: The upper 1880s view of Main Street, looking towards the river, shows a very different downtown, prior to the 1892 fire. The building on the left was the Masonic Hall and the two-story building three doors up from it, on the corner of Main and Second Streets, was the Western Hotel. The post-fire image shows a vacant lot, where the lodge hall once stood, a fire damaged hotel, and across the intersection, Union Hall (a.k.a. Gibson building).

200 BLOCK OF MAIN STREET CIRCA 1920 & 2018: The upper images show the Rio Vista Garage, Hotel Rio Vista, and across the intersection, Union Hall (AKA Gibson building). The garage was built in 1918 and has been occupied over the years by several automotive businesses, including: (Peterson's) Rio Vista Garage, from 1918 to 1921; Kerner Motor Co., 1921 to 1924; Rio Vista Garage (Holmes & Sons), 1924 to 1931; Rio Vista Automotive Sales (Fox & Mortensen), from 1924 to 1936; and lastly, Abel Chevrolet, from 1936 to 1966.

FLYING A SERVICE STATION/MCGAHEY REAL ESTATE 2019: The Associated Service Station, more commonly known as the Flying A Service Station, was constructed in the mid-1940s and continued to operate until the late 1960s. In 1972, San Joaquin First Federal Savings constructed the current structure on the property for a mobile bank, whereby an armored vehicle would back into the building, each morning, carrying the safe, etc. After the bank closed in 1985, several other businesses followed, before the current real estate office moved in.

PARADE 1964 & 2019: During the 1964 Bass Derby parade, the recently organized Rio Vista Fire Department Drill Team, under the direction of Val deFlores, displayed their closed order drill techniques in front of parade spectators. The Flying A Service Station (1940s-late 1960s), Braid's Home Furnishings (1939-2013), and Safeway (1929-early 1960s) businesses figure prominently in the background.

BRAID'S 1942/2018: In 1939, Romildo "Braid" Pezzaglia purchased two lots in the 300 block of Main Street and hired Fred Lavering, a local contractor, to construct a two-story building for his year-old business, Braid's Appliance Store. The main floor would house the business, while the second floor would contain a residence for the owner. The business moved into the building in March 1939, closing its doors on December 31, 2013. Currently the building is occupied by The Social Butterfly consignment store.

SKAGGS SAFEWAY GROCERY STORE AND SPROUSE-REIZ 5 & 10/CHIROPRACTIC OFFICE: 1929, the Skaggs Grocery Company contracted to have this 60 x 85-foot brick structure constructed. When completed, the building was divided into two stores. Two-thirds of the store was occupied by Skaggs Safeway while the remaining third was occupied by Sprouse-Reiz 5 & 10. Safeway eventually expanded, occupying the entire building, until the early 1960s when they closed and another locally owned grocery store, Food Fair, opened in its place.

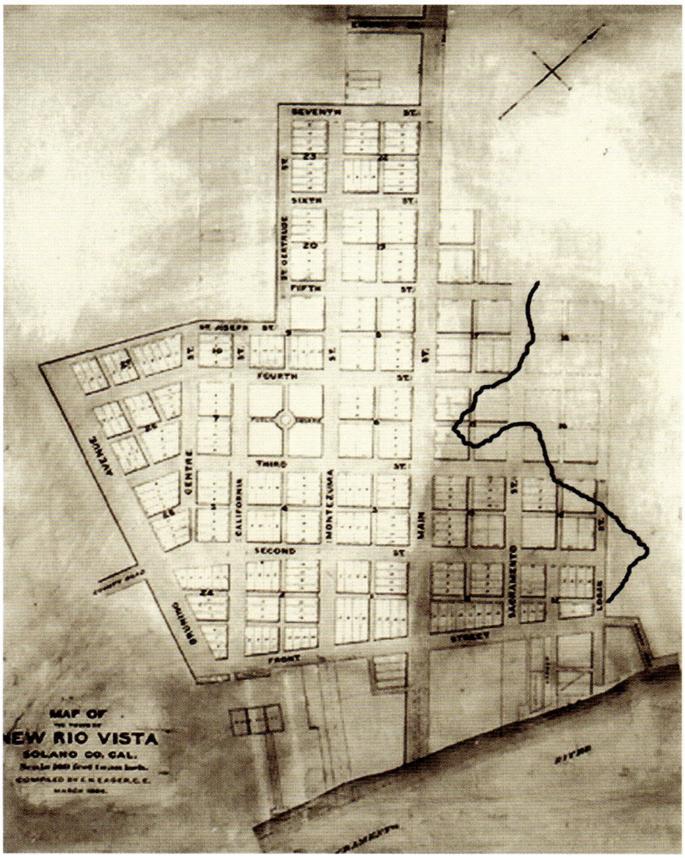

LAKE HOLDERSBACK/1886 MAP WITH OUTLINE OF LAKE: Lake Holdersback, sometimes referred to plainly as "the swamp," occupied the property where the present Rio Vista and Montezuma Fire Department buildings are located. The photograph was taken between 1901 and 1904 and shows the DeSoto home located on the corner of Main and Fourth Streets. A block up Main Street is the two-story home of the Chase family. The 1886 map shows the outline of the lake/swamp.

FIREHOUSE 1941 & 2019: The remodel of the 1926 Rio Vista firehouse was completed in September 1941, and that structure was used until 1976 when it was torn down and construction began on a new firehouse, which was completed in 1978. In 1950, the Montezuma Fire Protection district purchased the corner property, from the Soren Nielsen estate, and in 1951, the house was moved to Montezuma Street. In 1953, construction began and in March 1954, a formal dedication was held for their separate firehouse.

UNION BAPTIST CHURCH 1917 / WINDBORN CHURCH 2019: In July 1915, the Union Baptist Church of Rio Vista was organized under the direction of Rev. W. E. Story. In January 1917, the members voted to construct a church and when it was completed, in 1919, total expenditures were just under $25,000. Formally dedicated on April 20, 1919, the structure has remained a church since its construction; however, the denomination has changed several times.

CHASE HOSPITAL & DELTA PHARMACY 2018: The home of early pioneer and local merchant, James Chase, was built in 1874. After the Chase family moved out of the home, after the turn of the century, the home was converted into a hospital, as seen in this postcard. Eventually, the home was converted into apartments, which it continued to operate as until it was torn down in 1975. In 1979, the current building, the Delta Pharmacy, was constructed on the property.

DOZIER HOME & VACANT PROPERTY 2019: The 1868 members of the Dozier family, led by patriarch Anthony White Dozier, moved to Rio Vista from Georgetown, South Carolina. Soon after arriving, a large family home was erected on the southeast corner of Main and Fifth Streets. The home changed hands several times, being owned through the years by families including: Johnston, Tryon, Lent, and Bennett. By the mid-1950s, the house was starting to show its age, and it was decided by its owner to tear it down.

COOK HOME 1929/ 2002: Mr. and Mrs. Peter Cook purchased property on the southwest corner of Main and Fifth Streets, from Eugene Blanche Naulot Schneily, on December 5, 1905, for the sum of $10. The initial home was a small but modest one story to start with, eventually being enlarged to make it the stately brick two-story after about a decade. Little has changed since either of these two photographs were taken.

RIO VISTA BAND 1920S PARADE & TODAY: At one time, both sides of Main Street from Fourth Street were lined with stately two-story homes of prominent local pioneers. It was always a fitting backdrop to the host of parades and celebrations, such as this 1920s parade, which took place in Rio Vista. From left to right, the two-story homes of Brookes, Yorg, and Christensen can be seen. The Christensen home was torn down and two small houses were built in its place, in 1938.

Japanese Graves 1960s & 2010: When Morgan Tract was being developed in the late 1950s, a park was required as part of the new "Pleasant Hills" subdivision, which included Sierra Avenue and Morgan Lane. It was decided that the area, commonly referred to as the "Chinese Cemetery" (even though there are no Chinese buried there), could be outfitted with playground equipment and renamed Bruna Vista Park. A resolution was agreed upon whereas to give the proper respect to the "Japanese" tombstones, they would be laid flat and encased in concrete.

Vista Lanes 1968 & Family Dollar 2018: Built in 1963, the Vista Lanes offered a bowling alley, a bar, and a restaurant. A popular local hot spot during the 1960s and 70s, by the mid-1980s the building was sitting vacant and fell into disrepair. During the late 1990s, the building was torn down and Taco Bell/KFC erected a restaurant on a portion of the land. A few years later, in 2016, Family Dollar erected a building on the site between the restaurant and the cemetery.

WELCOME SIGN 1967 & 2018: The "Welcome to Rio Vista" sign and landscaping came about in late 1966. The Women's Improvement Club of Rio Vista choose to undertake the civic beautification project at the triangular plot of ground adjacent, to the west of the Mobil Service Station at the junction of Highway 12 and Main Street. At the time, the plot in question was barren and covered with Bermuda grass.

MOBIL SERVICE STATION EARLY 1960S & VACANT LOT 2018: In 1958, Mr. Crosby relocated his Shell service station, from the junction of Highway 12 and Front Street, to this piece of property located near the junction of Highway 12 and Main Street. The next owner turned it into a Mobil station. After the station was closed in 1983, the building was remodelled to house a delicatessen, followed by a Subway franchise. In 2009, the building was torn down and in recent years a mobile hot dog stand has been setting up daily on the property.

A&W 1960s & Medical Office 2018: On July 10, 1959, Bill Cumberland opened an A&W Root Beer Stand on Highway 12, next to the Mobile Service Station. For more than two decades, the business flourished and became the hangout for both teenagers and families. In 1981, Cumberland closed its order window for the last time. The building was shortly thereafter torn down and a bank building was erected on the site. That building still stands today, surviving two banks and a remodel into a medical facility.

Vista Motel 1955s & 2019: As the town continued to grow and the Triquero Tract was opened, in 1947, on the north side of Highway 12, the need for motels catering to the weary traveler presented itself. Opened in 1955, the Vista Motel continued to operate, under the same name, but different owners until 2008 when new owners changed the name to the Royal Inn. The second motel opened on Highway 12 was the Rio Sands Lodge in 1964, near the entrance to the bridge.

Herrick/Oilwell Materials & Hardware 2018:

This 1951 photograph depicts the local Cal Indians baseball team, sponsored by Herrick Tractor Company. The Indians were one of two "pre-little league"-era teams organized locally. Herrick, primarily a farm equipment company, closed during the early 1950s and in 1955 Jack Dole moved his hardware company, which he established in 1952, from Front Street into the former Herrick building on Highway 12.

Egbert Field Baseball Park 1971 & 2018: After twenty years of use, from 1939 to 1958, Sullivan & Larsen Baseball Park was showing its age, and it was decided to construct a new field adjacent to the recent housing developments on the north side of Highway 12. The official dedication for Egbert Field, named after local baseball enthusiast E. S. "Eggie" Egbert, took place on July 20, 1958, with more than 700 citizens in attendance for the opening-day ceremonies of the field, located on St. Francis Way.

VETERANS MEMORIAL BUILDING, CALIFORNIA STREET 1950S/ST. FRANCIS WAY 2019: The Veterans Memorial Building, located on the corner of California and Third Streets, was officially dedicated on January 29, 1928. Built for the Rio Vista Post No. 178 American Legion, the building would be utilized by future local veterans' organizations until it was destroyed by a fire in 1968, following a fire department dance. Two years later, the County approved $178,000 for the construction of a new building on St. Francis Way, which was officially dedicated on July 11, 1971.

HIGHLAND GOLF COURSE 1960S/TRILOGY 2019: In October 1962, work began on Rio Vista's Highland Golf Course, located on property owned by Duncan McCormack off Liberty Island Road. C. P. Beauchein, McCormack's father-in-law, designed both the course and the three-story clubhouse that housed a banquet room, cocktail lounge, pro shop, and coffee shop. On April 11, 1964, supervisor Raymond Church cut the ribbon that formally opened the nine-hole golf course. The course closed during the early 1970s and the clubhouse was torn down in the early 1980s.

FERRY *ALMA* 1890S AND FERRY *REAL MCCOY II* 2019: The *"Alma"* is an example of an early privately-owned ferry which catered to the day-to-day short mileage transportation moving farmers, equipment, and livestock from the mainland to Ryer Island. The state took over the ferry route in 1933 and in 1945 the *Real McCoy* was placed into operation. In 1962, it was changed to a non-cable deep water system allowing for ocean going vessels heading to Sacramento. In 2011, *The Real McCoy II*, was placed in service.

California Packing Corporation Plant #22/ Blackwelders: The Rio Vista Canning and Packing Company was formed in March 1904 and remained locally owned until 1918 when the California Packing Corporation, headquartered in San Francisco, purchased the plant and renamed it California Packing Corporation Plant #22. In the 1930s, this Del Monte brand facility was considered one of the largest asparagus canneries in the world. The plant closed in 1945 and in 1949, Blackwelder Manufacturing moved onto the property and setup in the vacated buildings.

Contra Costa Radiator 2015 and Fire Insurance Map 1941: In the time since Blackwelders closed in 1989, the buildings have been utilized by several businesses including Dutra, DDM, Contra Costa Radiator, and Barrier Systems. The 1941 map shows a portion of the California Packing Corporation Plant #22 compound, which besides normal plant operations also included employee housing, bathing facilities, social hall, nursery, play area, cafeteria, and double tank water tower.

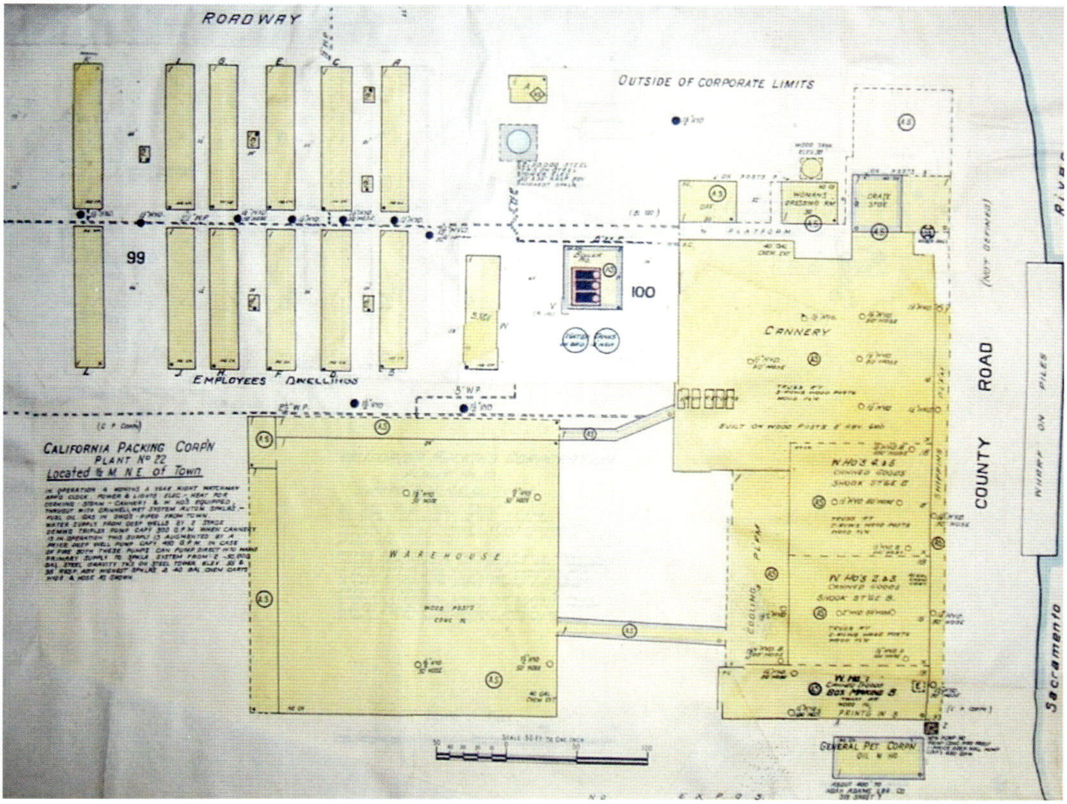

RIO VISTA FROM ABOVE 1965 AND 1972: Abel Chevrolet, Blackwelder's Iron Works, and Halliburton are prominent in the both aerial photographs. Other businesses visible on Highway 12 are: Rio Sands Lodge, Texaco, Shell, Standard and Union 76 Service Stations, Granny's Drive-In, P.G. & E., Caltrans, Oilwell Materials, and Savemart. It would be in the late 1970s that the fishing pier was constructed.

WATERFRONT EARLY 1960S AND 2019: The landscape has changed slightly in the nearly fifty years between the taking of these two photographs. During the 1960s, many businesses still utilized the waterfront, including Blackwelder's Iron Works and Dutra Dredging, leaving the remnants of several wharfs, which are still visible today. The "old" highschool, torn down in 1966, and the new city water tower, built in the early 1960s, are both visible on the horizon.

UNION OIL COMPANY 1920S: In April 1921, construction began on a standard type bulk distributing station, with wharf for the Union Oil Company on the south side of the Rio Vista Bridge. The plant was the largest between Sacramento and San Francisco and had two large tanks of 80,000-gallon capacity, for gasoline and distillate, and one 20,000-gallon tank for kerosene. The body of water visible was part of the swamp that was later filled in to create the "Sunnyside Terrace" subdivision during the 1950s.

Rio Vista Bridge 1959 and 2018: The “new” Rio Vista Bridge was built just 60 feet upstream from the older bridge. Construction took place in two phases: the eastern structure between 1943-1945 and the lift span and western portion between 1957-1960. In 1945, a “crossover” for traffic was constructed, attaching the two bridges. By this means, from 1945 to 1960, both bridges were used in combination via the “crossover,” thus taking advantage of the old bridge’s movable span and the new bridges completed section.

North Front Street 1962 & 2018: The November 1962 image looking north down Front Street towards the Rio Vista Bridge shows the cement plant, Dolk Tractor, onramp to the bridge, Rosie's Café, and Abel Chevrolet. The site that the cement plant was located on currently is utilized each year for the annual Bass Derby festival's carnival.

NORTH FRONT STREET CIRCA 1941 & 2019: A comparison of the two images, taken looking south down Front Street towards Main Street, shows a very different business district in the early 1940s compared to 2018. The earlier image shows Berglund Tractor and Equipment Co., Shell Oil, Roy Ish Motors and Gordon-Hansen Company, on the east side of the street, and Holz Tires on the corner of Front and Logan Streets. The Berglund and Shell buildings were torn down, the latter during the 1970s.

GORDON-HANSEN COMPANY 1940S & 2018: One local building which captures the architectural feel of the art deco era of the 1930s is the former Gordon-Hansen Company Ltd. Building, located on Front Street. The downtown landmark was constructed in 1938 and has been the home to only three businesses since its doors opened. For close to fifty years, the Gordon-Hansen Company occupied the building, followed by Dry Vac and then Preferred Windows. Oldtimers may remember the vertical sign and clock, which hung above the main entrance.

WALLACE PLUMBING & VACANT LOT 2019: By far one of the more unusual buildings which graced the downtown was the saloon and residence of Joseph Silva Vieira, built in 1899 on the northwest corner of Front and Sacramento Streets. The building originally was occupied by The Dewey Saloon on the main floor and the Vieira family's residence on the second floor. The building went through several owners until it was destroyed by fire in 1984. The last occupants were Wallace Plumbing and The Poppy Club.

NORTH FRONT STREET 1930S & TODAY: Looking north down Front Street, the upper image shows the Chop House, barber shop, Cavagnaro's Blacksmith Shop, The American Railway Express (Christensen building) U.P.E.C. Hall, and a saloon occupying the north side of the street and the Egbert properties across on the east side. Today, the former blacksmith shop is occupied by the Rio Vista Museum, the Christensen building by a certified public accountant, and the U.P.E.C. Hall by insurance and attorney offices, with a private club meeting upstairs.

BILL KING'S CHEVRON SERVICE STATION 1950s & HAP'S BAIT 2019: A service station occupied the corner of Front and Main Streets from the mid-1930s through the 1960s. The stations proprietorship changed several times, including owners Herlihy, King, Willis, Graham, and McKarley. The station was torn down in the late 1960s and Hap's Bait, which was adjacent and established in the 1950s, continued to operate gas pumps until the 1990s. The building next to the service station, which housed Moniz's plumbing business, was torn down and the lot is currently vacant.

RIO VISTA MUNICIPAL DOCK 1950s & 2019: In May 1949, on the approval of council, the city purchased pontoons and the rest of the materials and supplies to construct a 120-foot dock, which was completed at the foot of Main Street just in time for the re-established Bass Derby and Water Carnival, held in September of that year. In 1967, the dock was removed from the water and a complete reconditioning was performed. Most recently, the dock was replaced, in the summer of 2018.

CITY HALL 1950s & 2018: The Rio Vista City Hall was constructed for $60,000 and formally dedicated on October 8, 1950, during the annual Rio Vista Bass Derby and Water Carnival festivities. For several years prior, the city hall was in a section of the main floor of the Knights of Pythias Hall. The upper photograph shows Edgewater Drive had already been paved, but little home construction had been completed. At the far end of the street, Penney Brothers Boat Company's building can be seen.

PENNEY BROS. BOAT CO. 1950S & SOUTH END OF EDGEWATER DRIVE 2019: Harold and John Penney established Penney Bros. Boat Company in 1947, when they leased a portion of St. Joseph's Cut, which had previously been utilized as a cow pasture. The brothers cleared the land and erected a 40' x 100' building, for boat repair and established marine waterways and docking facilities. Eventually they leased the north side of "the cut" and part of the south shore, building docks and covered berths for sixty-five boats. The business closed in December 1959.

HUDSON AND SMITH 1941 & PARKING LOT 2018: For the past several decades, since the building was torn down, this lot on Main Street has been used as a parking lot for neighboring businesses. However, during the 1930s and 1940s, Mr. Hudson and Mr. Smith operated a successful automotive repair business on the site.

ST. JOSEPH'S MILITARY ACADEMY: From 1903 to 1932, St. Joseph's Academy for Boys (later augmented with the word "Military") graced the section of town which later became the "Riverside Subdivision," which includes Edgewater and Highland Drives, and the stretch of Bruning Ave. that connects them to Front Street. By 1923, the enrollment had increased substantially, and the good Sisters of Mercy decided to change the school to a military academy including, on faculty, a commandant with an army background as a male instructor.

SULLIVAN & LARSEN BASEBALL PARK: After St. Joseph's Military Academy closed in 1932, the former ball field continued to be maintained and used by the local high school. Since baseball had always been the town's favorite sport since the 1870s, in 1938 it was felt that the town finally deserved an official baseball field. The academy property owned by the families Sullivan and Larsen was an ideal for such an undertaking. The opening day festivities took place on May 11, 1939.

U.S. ARMY BASE 1970S/ ABANDONED BASE 2019: In 1911, U.S. Engineer Storehouse, Rio Vista, was established south of town on 28.1 acres. In 1952, after forty-one years of primary flood control usage, the base was reassigned from civilian to military jurisdiction and the base changed from flood control to storage and maintenance of army harbor craft. The height of operations was the year 1963, when a reported 300 civilians were employed at the base and 350 vessels were in storage. The base officially closed in 1991.

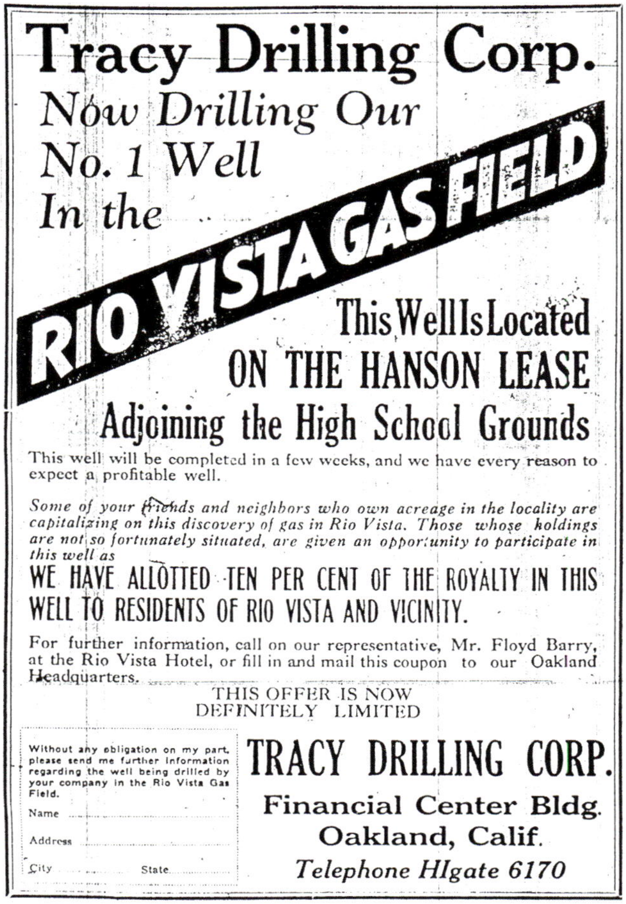

GAS INDUSTRY ADVERTISEMENT & TYPICAL GAS WELL: During the 1920s, several teams of geologists inspected the area and exploratory wells were drilled in 1921 and 1928. Unfortunately, those wells met with negative results. On June 18, 1936, two miles west of town, Amerada Petroleum Corporation brought in the first producing well. Initially, Amerada was drilling for oil when they discovered natural gas. At first, the people of Rio Vista did not realize what impact the gas industry would have on them, but they soon found out.

NOB HILL CIRCA 1910 AND TODAY: Second Street was just a dirt road when the upper photograph was taken to be used as a postcard. The caption referred to the section as "Nob Hill," however no one locally called it that prior to the photograph's release. Considered one of the most prominent neighborhoods of its time, the stately homes of Felix Drouin, Dr. A. J. McKinnon, Henry Dirr, and Senator Thomas McCormack lined the west side of the street.

SANTA CLARA STREET: Around the time that the Rio Vista Grammar School, seen in the background, was being constructed, many of the surrounding streets, such as Santa Clara Street, were paved for the first time, accommodating for automobiles as more local citizens were driving.

Rio Vista Grammar School Circa 1930/ Riverview Elementary 2011: The Rio Vista Grammar School, constructed on Second Street, was completed in 1918. Peter G. Jacobs was the first principal, a position he held until 1951, and the first graduating class consisted of twelve students. The school would choose blue and gold as their colors, adopt the panther as their mascot, and after several decades, change its name to Riverview. The main school building was destroyed in April 1971 by fire and replaced with a modern open floorplan building.

SECOND STREET AT THE TURN OF THE CENTURY AND TODAY: Looking up Second Street, towards Main Street, the intersection of Second and California Streets shows young trees and wooden sidewalks bordering a dirt road. It was not until 1917 that Second Street was paved, just prior to the completion of the grammar school. In the distance, the top of the Knights of Pythias Hall and the Sidwell Hotel water tower can be seen.

Masonic Hall 1950s & 2018: In May 1937, a motion was put forth that a new temple be constructed. For sixteen years various proposals were considered, but it wasn't until 1953 that construction began on a building, on the northwest corner of Second and California Streets. The building was completed in July 1954 and formally dedicated on August 14. For most of the thirty-seven years since their hall was destroyed by fire in 1917, the lodge had been meeting in the Knights of Pythias hall.

KNIGHTS OF PYTHIAS HALL/ RIO VISTA LIBRARY FIRE 1993: Rio Vista Lodge No. 165, Knights of Pythias, was chartered on October 11, 1889, with thirty-two members signing the charter. Seven years later, they erected a two-story building on the northwest corner of Second and Montezuma Streets. The hall, completed in August 1896, originally boasted a gymnasium and office on the main floor and meeting rooms on the second floor. After the turn of the century, a portion of the first floor was used as the city hall until 1950.

THE "OLD" AND THE "NEW" RIO VISTA LIBRARY: The interior photograph of the "old" Rio Vista library, taken in 1968, shows head librarian Mary Lee Hamilton updating the card file. In 1993, a fire broke out on the second floor and damage was such that the building was demolished, and the library moved into temporary quarters on Main Street. The Rio Vista branch of the Solano Library was established in 1914.

HOTEL SIDWELL/HOTEL SIDWELL BAR: John Sidwell erected the first hotel in Rio Vista on this property in 1862. Sidwell had no previous experience in the hotel business, but he saw a need for a hotel, and filled the need. He previously operated a general store, which he established in 1854, on Grand Island at Sidwell's Landing and then relocated to "old" Rio Vista. Sidwell continued to run his hotel up until his death in 1882 at which time his wife, Annie, took over operations.

HOTEL SIDWELL LATE 1920S & TODAY: After the devastating fire of 1892, Mrs. Sidwell was the first in town to commence work on a replacement structure. The new two-story hotel was built on the same site, with the ground floor measuring 30 x 58 feet and the second floor 30 x 44 feet. During the early 1900s a new section was added onto the front of the building. The hotel has operated under several names, including: Hotel Sidwell, The California Hotel, and Hotel Ram.

SIDWELL GARAGE 1930S & RIO VISTA MUNICIPAL PARKING LOT 2018: The Sidwell Garage, located on the northeast side property adjacent to the hotel, opened in 1915, The original tenant was Murray Isham, who brought in a partner, Joe Lorentz, during the late 1920s. From 1935 to 1948, Abel Chevrolet occupied the building. After Abel relocated to Main Street, they continued to use the building for the storage of automobiles. Eventually the city purchased the property, tearing down the building and making a Municipal Parking Lot.

LAURITZEN FRUIT STAND/ FORMER LAURITZEN HOME AND FRUIT STAND 2018: Robert Lauritzen's Fruit Stand was constructed next door to the Lauritzen family home, on Second Street, in December 1903 and operated until around 1935. Prior to its construction, Robert sold his goods from the family residence. Since the fruit stand closed, a handful of businesses including a dry cleaner, men's clothing store, photographer, beauty parlor, florist, second-hand store, and several cafés, have occupied in building. Robert emigrated, with his parents, from Denmark to California in 1868.

RIO VISTA YOUTH CENTER 1968 & 2018: In 1946, the local Boy Scout troops, who had no official place to meet, proposed the idea and need for a center to be built for the youth of the town. The local chapter of the Lions Club took on the project, naming W. H. "Krug" Dunbar chairman of the building committee. A combined dedication ceremony and Boy Scout District Court of Honor was held on Saturday, February 7, 1948, with a reported audience that held more than 400 persons.

FIRST CONGREGATIONAL CHURCH MARCH 22, 1899 AND 1940S: Rev. Solomon B. Dunton came to Rio Vista in 1867 and organized "The First Congregational Society of Rio Vista." The following year, John H. Gardiner donated two lots for a church site. The original church was erected in 1868, standing 45 feet by 30 feet and 16 feet high. The belfry tower stood 35 feet high, with the entrance facing east. The first service was held there on January 15, 1869.

FIRST CONGREGATIONAL CHURCH 1950S AND 2019: In 1899, the church incorporated as the First Congregational Church of Rio Vista. Twenty-six years later, the social hall was constructed to the west of the Church. That same year, the old church structure was remodeled, receiving a new roof, belfry, a brick façade, and stained glass. The sanctuary was changed so that the entrance was on the corner.

ST. JOSEPH'S PARISH 1870S & CIRCA 1905: St. Joseph's Parish Catholic Church was formally organized in Rio Vista in June 1868 and that same month the original church was erected. In those early years, St. Joseph's fell under the jurisdiction of the Suisun Parish. Father Lucovicus Alphonsus Auger was brought to town and became St. Joseph's first permanent priest. The church was constructed on land, located on Fourth Street, which was donated by Joseph Bruning, who also played a significant role in financing the project.

St. Joseph's Circa 1910 & 2019: The church was remodeled in 1904 to reflect the style of architecture referred to as "Carpenter Gothic," complete with stained glass windows, each with inscriptions dedicating them to prominent local catholic pioneers. To the left of the church were two homes owned by the Roman Catholic Church and used as a priest house and a rental. To the right is the Egbert home, and to the rear is St. Gertrude's Academy.

WOMEN'S IMPROVEMENT CLUB 1929 & 1968: In 1912, a group of local women organized a club with the intention of improving Rio Vista. In September 1920, the Woman's Improvement Club joined the State Federation of Women's Clubs and on March 23, 1928, a celebration took place formally dedicating their new clubhouse, on the corner of Fourth and Montezuma Streets. The club used the building until the 2000s when they sold it to a local men's club, which in 2017 sold it to a local church.

BRUNING SCHOOL 1930S AND 2018: The Bruning School was erected in 1929 as a primary school and continued to operate in that capacity until 1966, when the school district was reorganized and the building became the offices for the newly formed River Delta Unified School District. Originally the property was the site of the Public School, erected in 1862. The adjacent homes of were owned by W. H. Simpson, Mary Offerman, Henry Offerman, and Mary Gomez, at the time of the school's construction.

RIO VISTA HIGH SCHOOL 1939 & 2018: Rio Vista Joint Union High School was designed by architect A. R. Smith, who also designed Armijo High School in Fairfield and Dixon High School in Dixon. The cost of construction was approximately $100,000 and began in February 1915. As the enrollment grew, the campus grew with it, adding additional buildings in 1939 (39 wing), 1954 (Library-Cafeteria wing), and 1966 ("A" building, shop, gymnasium, agricultural, Football Bowl Field). The three-story original building was torn down in 1966.

TEACHERS HOUSES/VACANT LOT 2018: When Rio Vista Joint Union High School expanded by building a new wing containing a library, cafeteria, bathrooms, and hall, in 1953, several of the homes that were located on the property were moved to Drouin Lane, between Seventh Street and the bus garages. During the remaining 1950s, the 60s, and early 70s, the homes were utilized for housing teachers, eventually being torn down during the mid-1970s.

ACKNOWLEDGMENTS

In 1958, Rio Vista celebrated its 100 years of existence (1858-1958) with a nine month long Centennial celebration, during which time a temporary museum was set up in a storefront on Main Street. Dozens of photographs and artifacts were loaned by residents for the displays. Seventeen years later, as the country was celebrating its Bicentennial, many communities across the nation formed historical associations, including Rio Vista.

In 1975, a group of citizens gathered together and formed the Rio Vista Museum Association. The purpose of this association was to collect, safeguard, and publicly display documents, photographs, and objects of historical significance to the city of Rio Vista and its residents. The Rio Vista Museum, located at 16 North Front Street, is a must see for every resident and visitor to Rio Vista who would like to know a little more about this fine 161-year-old California town.

It is because of this local interest and vast photograph archives that I found myself faced with the difficult job of choosing the images to include in this book, as there were too many. I tried as often as possible to use images that have not been published or those that show buildings torn down many years ago. I believe that I picked the best of the best, and in doing so, have included some "hidden gems."